Dear L

Wonderful
with you!
I look forward to
seeing you again!

Warmest Regards,

10/23/2012

Victory Over Violence

Nancy's Story and The Business Of Me

Nancy Salamone

authorHOUSE®

AuthorHouse™
1663 Liberty Drive
Bloomington, IN 47403
www.authorhouse.com
Phone: 1-800-839-8640

First published by AuthorHouse   7/14/2010

ISBN: 978-1-4520-2509-4 (e)
ISBN: 978-1-4520-2507-0 (sc)
ISBN: 978-1-4520-2508-7 (hc)

Library of Congress Control Number: 2010909515

Printed in the United States of America
Bloomington, Indiana

This book is printed on acid-free paper.

Dedication

This book is dedicated to all women who have endured domestic violence; my mom, who I love very much; and to Dede Bartlett and Carole Hyatt, who have not only opened their networks but their hearts to help and mentor me.

And to M.B., who held my hand, gave me courage, wiped away my tears, and made me smile.

Contents

Nancy's Story

When things are tough,

just remember,

every flower that ever bloomed

had to go through a whole lot of dirt to get there!

… Anonymous

Nancy's Story

I'm Nancy, and I am going to tell you a story.

For twenty years, I kept a secret from my family and coworkers. The secret was that I lived two lives. One, a successful corporate executive and the other, a behind closed doors battered wife.

I'm a survivor of domestic violence. I was physically, emotionally, and economically abused by my husband.

My coping mechanism was a fantasy world that I created, one where life was good.

One of my favorite fantasies was that my husband was dead. Being a widow would be a wonderful thing, because it was acceptable to be a widow but not acceptable to be a divorced woman.

I kept my secret for twenty years, because I was ashamed.

Then, on December 28, 1991, I left.

I no longer know the Nancy who left, but I will always be grateful to that person inside me who finally summoned the courage to leave so that I could move on and thrive.

My hope is that women who have endured their own struggles find something from my story and realize that they too can create the financially self-sufficient life that they choose and achieve their own "Victory over Violence".

The Honeymoon Is Over

The Honeymoon Is Over

You may trod me
In the very dirt
But still,
Like dust,
I'll rise
… Maya Angelou

It was the very day we got home from our honeymoon. There I was, lying on the bathroom floor, naked and bleeding. He didn't like the way I hung the towels in the bathroom. When he was done, I had been beaten and sodomized and he was telling me that, "Women like anal sex," and asking what was the matter with me.

I was nineteen. That was the beginning of my marriage. The abuse—physical, sexual, emotional, and economic— would continue for twenty years.

My Early Years

What we remember from childhood we remember forever—permanent ghosts, stamped, inked, imprinted, eternally seen.
Cynthia Ozick,
American short-story writer, novelist, and essayist

How I Got There

I was born, the oldest of three girls, into a Sicilian, Roman Catholic family in the Bronx, New York.

My mother's family lived not far from us, and since she was one of ten children, I had a large group of aunts, uncles, and cousins.

I was told from a very young age that children should be seen and not heard. And I listened.

I was not a loud or rambunctious child. If someone told me to sit, I sat—quietly. My favorite places to sit were corners. To this day, I still prefer the corner of a couch.

My family was so large that you had to yell to be heard. But I was not a yeller, so I never said very much. The yelling was not always done from anger; many times, it was because it was the only way to be heard above the roar. Yelling was a way of life in my family.

A Four-Year-Old with Migraines

As a small child, I suffered from migraines. I would have tremendous head pain and could not move my head or open my eyes.

My mom took to me a lot of doctors, and I even had my head x-rayed. It was a strange thing to be so small and to lie on a table with a huge machine moving above my head.

It was finally decided that I was a nervous child, and I was given pills to calm me. I am not a therapist or psychiatrist, so I don't know what really caused my migraines. The only thing I do know is that I had them, and one day they just went away.

What I also know is that I never felt like I fit in. But I was always *trying* to fit in with everyone. I never really spoke up for myself and would follow the herd. I wanted desperately to be liked and a center of attention. But with so many cousins, it was hard for me to shine because I was so withdrawn.

My dad was many years older than my mom, and being Sicilian, he wanted sons. Unfortunately for him, my two sisters, and me, he had girls. Dad told me once, "You're girls, so you are your mother's problem. If I had sons, I could do things with them, but I have girls." It still makes me sad when I think about what he said. He wrote us off. We were girls, and because we were girls, he didn't want to spend any time with us.

Don't Ever Tell Anyone You're Pretty

My mom did everything. She worked, she cooked, she cleaned, and she altered our clothes. One day when I was about five, Mom was altering one of my dresses. Standing in front of a mirror, I really liked what I saw. I thought I was really pretty.

"I'm beautiful," I said to my mom. My mother snapped at me, "Never say that again. You sound conceited."

I didn't know what conceited meant; after all, I was only five years old. But the lesson I learned was that it wasn't a good thing to feel good about yourself.

My First Day of Kindergarten

My mother enrolled me in Immaculate Conception School. All of my cousins went there, too.

Kindergarten was half day, and I was enrolled in the morning session. I wore a pretty pink dress for my first day at school.

My mom drove me to school and walked me to the classroom and left. There I was.

The classroom was set up with small round tables and chairs. I was told to sit at a table with the other little kids. Separation anxiety ran rampant! All the kids were crying. I didn't. I did as I was told and sat quietly.

I have never told anyone about this before. Like the other kids, I must have been very frightened, but I didn't cry. But I did soil my panties. And even after I did, I never said a word.

All of a sudden, the kids at my table stopped crying and turned to stare at me. I knew why. I stunk!

The nun came over and asked me to leave the classroom. She called my mother, who had to bring me clean clothes. I remember being cleaned in the school bathroom and then going back to my seat. I never cried.

My First Confession

I was in first grade when I made my first confession.

A first confession was made before making a first communion. Before making a first communion, you had to be free of sin—in other words, confess your sins and be granted forgiveness.

The school was associated with the Immaculate Conception Church. I was six years old when I, together with all of my classmates, made my first confession. On the appointed day, the nuns marched us to the church. I always thought it was dark and dank in the church. It was a scary place to me.

We all lined up against the church pews, waiting for our turn to go into the confessional box. The nuns told us we had to confess all of our sins, and we had to give an accounting of how many times we committed each one of them. For example, if your mother yelled at you because you did something wrong, you had to confess how many times she yelled at you.

When it was my turn, I entered the confessional box, which was even darker than the church. In fact, it was pitch-black in there. A small window opened, and it was my time to talk. "Bless me, Father, for I have sinned. This is my first confession, and my mother yelled at me four times, and I was mean to my sisters three times." I went on like this for what seemed an eternity until I finished. The priest then told me to say five Hail Marys and one Our Father, and off I went, to do as I was told and glad to be out the confessional box.

I was six years old and scared to death. And yes, I lied to the priest, as I had no idea how many times I got yelled at or how many times I might have been mean to my sisters.

Every Friday after my first confession, we were marched off to church to confess our sins once again. I had a rule: I would never admit that I ever sinned more than five times. I don't know why five, but I must have felt that any sin committed fewer than five times was not that bad.

So much for what I learned about confession…

I Hate the Cold

I hate being cold. I'm not sure why. But there was an incident that happened in grammar school that might explain it.

It was routine at school that we all lined up in the yard with our class each morning by a certain time. I really don't remember what time, but it was early, something like eight o'clock, I think. The nuns would come to open the school doors at a specific time, and as we were trained to do, we would march into our classrooms. The truth was that you could set your watch to the time the nuns opened the doors every morning.

One particularly frigid Bronx winter morning, the nuns didn't show up on time to open the doors. We were very obedient little children, trained like soldiers and lined up in our straight lines, waiting in the cold to get into the school.

I don't know how long we stood there, but for a small kid who was freezing, it seemed like forever. Then, finally, the nuns opened the door.

I don't remember ever getting a reason why they were not there on time or an apology for keeping us waiting, but as I was taught, "Children should be seen and not heard." They never explained, and I never asked.

Omertà

Omertà is a popular attitude and code of honor common in areas of southern Italy (such as Sicily), where criminal organizations like the Mafia are strong. A common definition of "omertà" is "code of silence."

A common misconception is that the Mafia created omertà. In fact, the code was adopted by Sicilians long before the emergence of the Cosa Nostra. Some date omertà to the sixteenth century, when it was used as a way of opposing Spanish rule. To this day, for generations of Sicilians, this code is alive and operative.

I can absolutely affirm that omertà is alive and well in my Sicilian family. In fact, my sisters and I were never told my dad's real age.

Dad was twenty-one years older than my mother, and he didn't want us to know. Obviously, my mother knew, and so did my aunts, uncles, and cousins, but not us. Omertà works.

One day, my parents were having a screaming match in the kitchen, and my sisters and I were in the living room, sitting quietly and waiting for it to end. All of a sudden, we heard my mom yell out my dad's real age, which was ten years older than what we had been previously told. My sisters and I just stared at each other, thinking that Mom had made a mistake. But then we heard Dad say that he was proud of his age and then we were really confused.

We also found out that day that my dad was divorced, and our mother was his second wife.

Omertà prevailed in my home. The "code of silence" kept us from learning about anything that anyone else felt might embarrass the family. We would only learn many of my dad's other secrets in the years to come.

So, I guess part of the reason I never told anyone about my abused life was some part of my Sicilian background, which instructed us to, "Carry your cross in silence," and don't tell anyone anything that might embarrass you or your family. And that's what I did.

The Idioms I Was Brought Up Wit

"Carry your cross," "You make your bed, you lie in it," and, "Don't hang out your dirty laundry," are the idioms I heard as a kid, over and over again, when I had a problem.

No one ever explained these idioms to me, so I had to create my own definitions.

Nancy's definition for "Carry your cross": life is tough, and no one really cares about your problems, so keep them to yourself.

Nancy's definition for "You make your bed, you lie in it": you made your choices, and you have to live with them. If you are not happy, it's your problem. Deal with it, because there's no going back.

Nancy's definition for "Don't hang out your dirty laundry": keep your secrets. No one should know about any problems that may embarrass you or your family.

Witches

When I was a child, I hated the dark. To this day, I don't understand why, and I don't remember when that fear left me.

I shared a bedroom with one of my sisters, and when the lights went out, I would think witches were outside the door, waiting to pounce on me. Yes witches—complete with black gowns, weird hats, and big, ugly noses. In fact, now that I think about it, the witches looked just like the Wicked Witch of the West in the movie, *Wizard of Oz*, with Judy Garland. The witch in that movie, with her screechy voice, scared the heck out of me.

These witches came every night to haunt me for years, and I haven't a clue why. Maybe it was the movie that stayed with me.

It always took a long time for me to get to sleep, because I was waiting for the witches to leave. Eventually, I did fall off, usually scared that I would be taken to a witch's lair.

The Bride of Frankenstein

Bride of Frankenstein was a 1935 horror movie starring Boris Karloff as Frankenstein's monster and Elsa Lancaster as his monster bride. The light in this movie was what I call "spooky light," the kind meant to scare you.

My mom and dad both worked, and my sisters and I were sometimes left in the care of an aunt, one of my mother's sisters. I never liked being at my aunt's house.

My aunt had four children, who are all older than I: three boys and a girl. One rainy Saturday we were stuck in the house, and my aunt put on the television to entertain us. One of my cousins insisted we watch *Bride of Frankenstein*. It was his home, so that's we watched.

I must have been around seven years old, and the movie scared me. To make matters worse, my cousin saw that I was scared and taunted me throughout the movie. The more frightened I became, the more he taunted, and the other kids began taunting me, too.

I hated that movie. It was the first horror movie I was forced to watch and the only one I have ever seen.

Kids are kids, so I don't blame him or my other cousins, but when my mom came to pick us up, I was ready to bolt out of their house.

I guess that movie made a real impact on me, as I woke up screaming from a nightmare about it that night.

I remembered this incident when *Bride of Frankenstein* was on TV the other night. Actually, this time I found it quite funny!

Knuckles—A Sadistic Card Game

Knuckles, or Bloody Knuckles, is a card game and a sadistic one at that. The object of the game is to have the lowest score. The person with the lowest score wins and gets to "bloody" the knuckles of the loser by hitting them with the cards.

My cousins and I played Knuckles, and if children could be mean, they were. I remember losing one time, and one of my cousins put the deck of cards on my hand and stomped his foot on it. Needless to say, I had bloody knuckles.

I get angry when I think of this, and I am not sure at whom. One part of me is angry at me for not standing up for myself, and the other is angry at my cousins for taking delight in hurting me. Perhaps I was a sensitive child, or maybe I just had no backbone.

My Middle Years

You couldn't get hold of the things you'd done and turn them right again. Such a power might be given to the gods, but it was not given to women and men, and that was probably a good thing. Had it been otherwise, people would probably die of old age still trying to rewrite their teens.
Stephen King, Author

We Meet

When I was a teenager, I spent my summers at Orchard Beach in the Bronx. My mom and dad worked, and we were old enough to take care of ourselves, so on many summer days, we were off to the beach. The "cool" section for teenagers was section thirteen, so that's where I went with my cousins and my little sister in tow.

Standing on the beach boardwalk one day when I was fifteen, this gorgeous guy walked by with a girl on each arm. He was tall, dark, and handsome. I was infatuated. Later that same day, he left the two girls behind and approached me. He was in college, and I was a sophomore in high school. I thought that it was really cool a college guy was interested in me.

After that meeting, we met again in my neighborhood and started dating. He was my first and only boyfriend.

He was a gorgeous guy, but moody and complex, and I was really attracted to him. I fantasized that I could make him happy. Ha!

His moodiness would become worse, and he took his unhappiness out on me. I stuck it out, because I continued to think I could fix it, as if I had some magical power. Of course I was wrong! But he was in college. He was older and handsome, and as I said, I was infatuated.

The Scarlet Letter

Being a "good Catholic girl" from a good Catholic family and good Catholic schools, I was indoctrinated with the idea that having sex was wrong unless you were married.

After my boyfriend and I had sex for the first time, I felt like I had sinned and that everyone could tell what I had done. It felt as if there was, like on Hester Prynne in *The Scarlet Letter*, a big red A on my chest that all could see. I was scared and confused. I was sixteen.

I thought I had done something *really* bad, and now I was afraid of being found out. This fear consumed me. Fear of things that I imagined *might* happen became my constant companion.

After we had sex the first time, we began bickering and fighting. Now that I look back on it, part of the reason for the fighting was that I was resentful, because I had not been ready to have sex yet. He had continually pressured me about sex, and I finally succumbed to that pressure.

After that, in spite of his moodiness, I stayed because by then, I felt like I was "tainted goods." I felt that no one else would want me.

When he finally asked me to marry him, I was relieved. I was not in love—I was relieved.

I was nineteen when I married him. The scarlet letter went away but not the fear. I had been pushed into a life I didn't want rather than pulled by a vision of what I wanted my life to be.

My mind was like a kaleidoscope; when one fear went away, another would flip right into place. The fear was constant and relentless.

My Fifteenth Birthday

Of course, we always got presents for our birthdays. My mom always tried very hard to get us what we wanted.

On my fifteenth birthday, she really surprised me though. I don't remember the gift, but I do remember that she picked me up from school that day and took to me to get a work permit. Not only did she get me a work permit, she also got me a job! Mom had arranged for me to work in our dentist's office.

I enjoyed working. The dentist employed mostly high school and college students, and our work schedules were designed around our school schedules. Not bad.

I loved learning and earning money. At work I learned responsibility, how to deal with the public, and how to be a team player.

I was a success at work. I earned responsibility quickly and knew that I was trusted by my boss and coworkers. Work was a place where I learned self-confidence.

Work was already a haven from the fear I would carry around for so many more years to come.

How I Met Dr. Zuckerman

One of the part-time dental assistants in the office was a really gorgeous older girl named Patty. Patty was a newlywed, and

I thought that she was very hip. It was 1969, and she had that very cool sixties' look with long, straight, dark hair; very cool bell-bottom jeans: and great hats. She was also very open about talking about sex. I had never met anyone like her.

One day while we were cleaning one of the examination rooms, she asked me if I had a boyfriend. When I said yes, Patty asked me if we were having sex. Again, I told her yes. She then asked me if I had seen a gynecologist, and when I said no, Patty was horrified. She told me that if I was having sex, I needed to see a gynecologist. I told Patty that I didn't know one. Patty told me that she had a great gynecologist in Manhattan and that his name was Dr. Zuckerman. She told me that I needed to make an appointment immediately. I followed Patty's advice and made an appointment with Dr. Zuckerman for more than a month away, the first appointment that I could get.

My First Appointment with Dr. Zuckerman

Dr. Marvin Zuckerman's office was on 86th Street and Park Avenue in Manhattan.

I was a kid from the Bronx, whose only experience with a doctor was our family doctor, Dr. Costa.

Dr. Costa was an old-fashioned family doctor who still made house calls. He was the doctor for my entire family, including my immediate family and my aunts and uncles and all of my cousins.

Dr. Costa had a small office in the Bronx, the only doctor's office that I'd ever really known. I didn't know what to expect when I walked into Dr. Zuckerman's office.

Dr. Zuckerman's office was beautiful. It was decorated with underwater photographs and other pieces of expensive artwork. I would later find out that Dr. Zuckerman owned a boat and took all the underwater photos himself.

I was seventeen when I had my first appointment with him.

When I arrived at the office, the nurse said that I should wait in the waiting room, which looked more like a beautifully appointed and comfortable living room to me. There was plenty of artwork to look at and a lot of great magazines to read. It was a good thing, too, because I would be doing a lot of waiting for Dr. Zuckerman over the years, as Dr. Marvin Zuckerman was the kind of doctor who never rushed a patient. He gave each patient the time and care that each needed.

After waiting for over an hour, the nurse finally called my name and escorted me into Dr. Zuckerman's office. Dr. Zuckerman's private office was just as beautifully decorated as the rest of the office; it was gorgeous.

I waited a few minutes, and finally, in walked this very tall man. He had long, dark hair pulled back in a ponytail.

He introduced himself and asked me why I was there to see him.

What I told Dr. Zuckerman was the boldest thing that I had ever told anyone in my life. I told him that I was having sex with my boyfriend and that I needed to be sure I did not get pregnant. Dr. Zuckerman said he would examine me, and after the examination, we would talk again.

His nurse came in, escorted me to an examining room, and instructed me to take off my clothes from the waist down and wrap myself in the examining cloth that she handed me. She told me I was to sit on the examining table and wait.

I did as I was told, and finally, Dr. Zuckerman came in and asked me to lie down. His nurse was with us in the room during the entire examination. I had already had intercourse a few times but never had anyone shined a spotlight on my vagina! This was all really new to me.

He put on rubber gloves and did an internal exam and then I felt a small amount of pain. Dr. Zuckerman said he was also doing a Pap test, and that was the reason for the momentary pain.

He finally shut off the light (the one shining on my vagina) and said to get dressed and meet him in his office.

Dr. Zuckerman was waiting for me. I already liked this man a lot.

Dr. Zuckerman informed me that the internal was fine, and he would let me know about the Pap test results when they came in. He then opened a drawer and handed me a package of birth control pills and instructed me about how to use them. He also gave me a prescription and told me that I should see him every six months for checkups.

That day began a relationship with Dr. Zuckerman that lasted for thirty-five years.

My ex-husband (still boyfriend at the time) told me he didn't understand why I needed to see a gynecologist, and we would argue about it every time I had an appointment.

I always enjoyed seeing Dr. Zuckerman. He always treated me with respect and great care, something that I did not get elsewhere in my life. He would later be instrumental in helping me realize that I needed to leave my marriage.

My Marriage

Turn your wounds into wisdom.
… Oprah Winfrey

I Couldn't Cook

About a month after we were married, I invited my youngest sister over for dinner one night. My youngest sister is six years younger than I am, so she was thirteen years old at that time.

I had spent the day cooking. I made my own tomato sauce; I made meatballs and a salad and had purchased a dessert. I was nineteen and had never really cooked much before. I thought I did a really good job and was feeling good about the meal that I made.

I felt good, that is, until my ex-husband tasted the meal and promptly declared it "disgusting" and threw everything that I'd cooked into the garbage. Yes, to my little sister's shock and my horror, he threw it all out. I was told that I was the worst cook ever, and the next time I cooked, I needed to be sure it was a meal worth eating.

I did cook over the years of my marriage. In fact, I also worked full time, while most of the time he was unemployed. I cooked, I cleaned, I worked, and he gambled.

He Managed the Money

As a kid, money was never discussed in our house, and for the twenty years of my marriage, my ex-husband completely dominated control of our finances.

Although I was the household's major wage earner, every payday I turned over my entire paycheck to my ex-husband. He told me how much money I could have and made me account for how much I spent from our account. I could never go shopping unless I had his permission and told him what I was going to purchase before I bought it.

Mom, I'm Unhappy

One evening, after I had been married for about two years, I went to the movies with my mom. While we were standing in line waiting to buy our tickets, I suddenly said to her, "Mom, I'm unhappy." Her reply was simply, "You made your bed, lie in it."

My mom endured her own unhappiness for many years. She and Dad hadn't gotten along for a very long time. In fact, they had not even shared the same bedroom for many years. It was a very sad, unhappy relationship, and she had suffered a lot.

I never again said anything to anyone about my unhappiness. My mom never knew about the abuse I endured until eighteen years later, when I finally summoned the courage to leave.

Dad and I Finally Talk

My dad and I were never close. He felt that we were girls, so we were my mom's "problem" (his word, not mine). He had little to do with our upbringing, and never spent much time with us. I always felt that he abandoned us.

Dad and I never had any father-daughter talks, nor did we ever spend much time together. I was rejected by the first male relationship I had.

It was our custom that the entire family always gathered together on Christmas Eve. On Christmas Eve 1982, we all gathered my aunt's house.

After the festivities, I went to my parent's house, and my dad did something unusual: he asked me to have a drink and talk to him. I was twenty-nine, and this was the first time we ever sat down together just to chat. I don't know what I drank or what we talked about, but I do remember Dad smiling at me and expressing happiness in having me there.

Dad told me that he was not feeling well. He told me that he was having indigestion. I will always remember the wonderful smile he had on his face as he talked to me. For the first time in many years, I kissed my dad before I left.

I was never to see him again. The following morning, he had a massive heart attack and died on the sidewalk while he was jogging. Dad was eighty.

It still hurts to think that perhaps we were finally developing a relationship and that he was taken away when he was. I loved my dad and only wanted his acceptance.

I Dazzled My Coworkers

I couldn't cook or clean according to my ex-husband, but I could dazzle my co-workers. I was the can-do person in the office. The office was the only place where I was respected, received praise, and felt rewarded.

One of my responsibilities was to organize and manage the company conferences. In the insurance industry, conferences are one way that companies bring their top producers together in one location to both reward and educate them.

Part of managing a conference was to prepare and ship all the conference materials to the conference location, so they were received and ready prior to the start of the event. It was not unusual for us to ship at least three airline containers full of materials.

We had scheduled a pick-up date for a conference. The day before the materials were to be shipped, there was a major blackout in New York City; the entire Wall Street area was without electricity.

But that didn't stop me. I had the entire staff that needed to be in the office in the office to be sure the shipment was sent out that day. The airline was sending the truck at 1 PM sharp, and the boxes had to be on the loading dock by that time.

My offices, and the materials, were on the eighth floor of the building, so the task of actually getting everything to the loading dock was not going to be an easy one. We purchased lanterns to light the stairwells and every able person carried boxes down eight flights of stairs and then walked back up to take more boxes down again.

The bottom line is that we made it, and the materials were delivered on time. My attitude at work was, "Get on the wagon, or get out of my way."

Yes, there were two Nancys: the can-do person, who could make things happen at work, and the behind-closed-doors-abused-wife.

I loved going to work, and that was the only thing I loved doing during my entire married life. Unlike others who could not wait for the weekend, I dreaded them.

I Hated Going Home

Most people liked it when the workday ended. Not me. I hated going home. I was afraid of how I would be greeted when I came through the door.

If I were lucky, all he would do was yell at me for about an hour and then go out. Other times, he would stay home and yell, scream, hit, and terrorize me.

On the nights that he would yell for what seemed like hours, I would sit quietly on the corner of the couch, my knees bent, my arms around my legs, and my head resting on my knees.

Some nights he would terrorize me by opening our apartment window. We lived in a unique building in Brooklyn, and although we were twelve floors up, the windows were twelve feet by twelve feet. He would go out on the ledge and threaten to jump.

One night, I heard a gunshot come from the kitchen. Later that evening, he came over to me and put that thing in my hand and told me to pull the metal trigger. I ran out of the apartment. I later found out it was a zip gun.

Home is supposed to be a haven; mine wasn't.

"I Can Have You Put Away"

"I can have you put away," my husband repeatedly told me. He was intimidating me, and because I was so traumatized, I bought every word of it.

I always worked late into the evening. One particular night, he was furious with me for coming in late. I was the major wage earner, and if it weren't for my salary, we would have lived on the street.

As soon as I came through the door, he started on me. "You're a lousy wife," he said. "You don't do anything a good wife does. You like wearing the pants in this marriage," he continued. And on and on it went. He finally told me to take off the jewelry that he had given me (in the twenty years we were married, he gave me an engagement ring and a wedding band, and we both paid for the wedding bands!) and put it on the bed. I did as I was told.

He told me I did not deserve to wear those rings and that he could have me put away. He told me since he was my husband, he could have me put away, and no one could stop him. I didn't know where "away" was, but I believed him.

He took my rings that night, and for a long time, he wouldn't give them back to me.

I felt good not wearing them.

Hold for Dr. Zuckerman

"Hold for Dr. Zuckerman," she said to me when I answered my phone at work one day. I recognized his nurse Lilly's voice. I had gone for my routine annual exam and Pap test the previous week. I had been having gynecological care for twenty years, and I had never had any issues.

Dr. Zuckerman came on the phone and said, "Nance [he always called me "Nance"], we have a problem. Your Pap test came back, and you have HPV with condyloma, and I need to do a biopsy." I was stunned.

I had the biopsy, which confirmed the original diagnosis of HPV (human papilloma virus). Dr. Zuckerman called me and told me to come to his office to talk about how to treat it.

He was a direct, no-nonsense person, and when I saw him in his office, he said, "Nance, there is only one way that you got this. It was sexually transmitted. This is not something you got from a toilet seat." He then said, "I know you, and I am telling you that you need to get your husband checked."

Those words kept haunting me, because without saying so directly, he was telling me that my husband had given me a very serious STD.

This was just a different form of abuse. I had been physically, emotionally, and sexually abused for years, and now I had found out that I was being abused by his dangerous sexual activity. This was 1989, and AIDS was rampant, so who knows what I could have contracted from him?

Going home on the train, I was sick to my stomach, and I was scared to death of what his reaction would be when I told him that he needed to see a doctor. I was more afraid of him than I was of the disease that he had given me.

When I got home, I told him that he needed to get checked. He refused. He yelled and slapped me around and told me that I should never have gone to the doctor in the first place. He told me that I probably got the STD from the doctor's dirty instruments.

When I asked Dr. Zuckerman if it was possible that I picked up the HPV in his office, he looked at me in his kind and gentle way and said, "Nance, there is only one way you got this—it was sexually transmitted."

The Treatment

The treatment for HPV was laser surgery. Dr. Zuckerman performed the surgery in his office and instructed me to come back in two weeks to see how I was doing.

Two weeks later, I was healing and he said he needed to do another Pap test in two months to see if the laser surgery had gotten it all.

Unfortunately, the laser surgery did not get all the infection, and I had to have what is known as a cervical conization, which is invasive surgery done in a hospital. The pain was excruciating.

My husband still did not get checked, and when I told Dr. Zuckerman, he said that I should not have intercourse with him unless I was protected.

We never had intercourse again. That was about nine months before I finally left him.

A Caring Friend

The night that I came home from the hospital, a male coworker called me at home to see how I was doing. My husband answered the phone and became enraged at me. I was in horrible pain, and now I was being accused of sleeping around and deserving everything I got.

My friend, Paul, never knew what he started. Paul was and is a very caring person, a devoted husband and father and good friend. Paul was just concerned about his friend and coworker: me.

Leaving

The first step to getting somewhere is to decide that you are not going to stay where you are.

… John Pierpont Morgan

My New Day

We all have our own morning routines. Some of us get up and do some exercise, and some of us enjoy some coffee and breakfast with our families and then off we go to get showered and dressed for our day.

The first thing that I did when I looked in the mirror every morning was to say to myself, "Tomorrow will be a better day." At 6 AM every day, I had already determined that

I was going to have a bad day, but as I was walking out the door, I would say to myself, "You can always leave."

I Left

December 28, 1991, was my "new day," because that was the day I left him.

To this day, I don't know who the Nancy was that left. It was an out of body experience. I felt like I was in a movie.

He was not there. I saw a woman packing a bag. I saw that person close the door behind her, suitcase in hand. I went to my mother's house.

When I arrived unannounced that Sunday evening, Mom opened the door, and before she could say a word, I said to her, "Have I got a story for you."

That week I did two things. First, I found myself an attorney, and next, I found a therapist. Or maybe it was the other way around. I don't remember. But, for the first time in my life, I was on my own and more scared of him than ever before.

Staying in an abusive marriage was difficult enough, but leaving was even more frightening. Once I left, a new reign of terror began in earnest. Not just against me but against my mother and my coworkers, too. I was constantly harassed by him at work.

At that time, I was the only female executive officer at the company, and he began to call my male counterparts and threaten to kill them—and me. I was so frightened that I hired a bodyguard to protect my mother and myself.

Thankfully I could afford protection. Many women in similar situations do not have the financial means to protect themselves adequately. We hear about those women all the time.

My Mom

My mom is a great woman. Over the years, I learned a lot from her. We haven't always agreed, but she has only wanted the best for me. When I needed her the most, the evening that I arrived at her doorstep unannounced, she was right there for me as she is today.

Mom is beautiful, and when she was young, she was gorgeous. I have the pictures to prove it! She was brought up during the Depression, and that framed her thinking in many ways. She believed in education and always wanted us to get good grades. She would yell at us if we didn't get good grades, and she had strict rules about what was acceptable and what was not. As a matter of fact, one standing rule was that if I got below a 70 percent on any school test, I shouldn't come home!

She needed to work after she got out of high school, so she went to beauty school and became a beautician. My dad was her first boss.

Since my dad was quite a bit older than she, and he got ill when she was a young mother, she was forced to go back to work and manage the beauty salon while raising three young kids. She was an early feminist and probably did not know it! She worked, she took care of my sisters and me, and she ran a business all at the same time. Many nights when she came home from work, she would sit at the dinner table and do her bookkeeping while she was eating dinner. Mom was tireless.

I learned from her how important it is to be good at your job and to appreciate the discipline needed to succeed. She is fiscally conservative and taught us that you needed to save money so that you have it when you need it. To this day (she is eighty-six years old), she has always been able to provide for herself.

Most important, she was my champion when I finally left my ex-husband. And as much as she did not want me to move out of her house, when the time came, she knew how important it was for me to have my own life. Mom actually found the ad for what would become my first apartment in Manhattan.

After my divorce, Mom became a great traveling companion. We have traveled together to Europe and visited places in the United States and always have had a great time.

Mom loves me, and I know that she is always there for me when I need her.

The Night I Thought I Would Die

He had moved out of the apartment we had shared and told my attorney that he was living out of state. I had not heard from him for a few weeks, and I finally felt comfortable enough to move back to the apartment. That was a bad decision. About two nights later, I heard the door open. He was in a rage.

He quickly came across the room and threw me against a closet door. I landed on my back. The next day, I noticed the door had been cracked. My back was also bruised and stayed that way for weeks.

Then he picked me up, threw me on the couch, and got on top of me. He started to squeeze my throat. His hands continued to choke me, and I closed my eyes and willed myself to relax and thought, *This is it; I am going to die, so just relax.*

I don't know why, but he finally stopped and left the house.

I sat on the corner of the couch, not moving for a long while. Then, like a robot, I began to clean up the mess created by his rage.

He had thrown wine bottles against the walls, so I cleaned the walls and swept up the glass. And when I was finished, I went to bed with a carving knife in my hand. I left on all of the houselights, too. He never came back that night.

Soon thereafter, I was diagnosed with post-traumatic stress syndrome.

"Nance, I Dreamt You Died"

The next day, I went to work as usual, but emotionally, I was a wreck. As I walked down the street to my office on Wall Street, my friend Marty saw me and started excitedly calling my name.

As Marty got closer, I could hear him say, "Nance, Nance, I had a dream about you last night. I dreamt that you died." As Marty got closer to me, the smile on his face evaporated, and he said in a stunned voice, "What happened to your neck?"

My neck was covered with welts and bruises. Like a journalist reporting the news, I unemotionally told him what happened. I had no emotions or feelings that morning. I was just a shell of a person.

Once in my office, I just sat there. I didn't answer the phone or read my mail; I didn't even turn on the computer. I just sat there, blankly staring at the wall in front of me.

A little while later, Marty came into my office and shut the door. He begged me to call my therapist, but I couldn't move. I just looked at him and didn't say anything.

My assistant came into my office and insisted that I get some food, but I didn't want to eat. So, Wilma took it upon herself and got me some food, which just lay there.

My boss, seeing the state I was in, insisted that I call my bodyguard and go get some clothes from my apartment and find another place to live.

I listened to all of them, and finally, I called my therapist, who insisted I see her that day. I went to see her, and she convinced me to do as my boss suggested and get some clothes and find a place to stay for a few days.

I called my sister, who was by then married and living with her husband in New Jersey. I asked if I could stay with her for a night, and she said sure. My boss insisted that I call a car service (which the company paid for) and go to my sister's house. I did as I was told. I didn't have the will to do anything else.

I never slept another night in that apartment.

So, You're Cured Now!

As I said, one of the first things that I did when I left was to get a therapist. To that point in my life, I had lived in secrecy, but I decided from that point forward I would live honestly. No more lies, no more secrets. I decided to tell the complete truth about everything to everyone all of the time.

I was staying with my mom, so before I left for work that day, I told her that I would be home a bit later than usual that evening, as I had an appointment with a therapist. Mom didn't say anything except that she would be home when I got in.

After work, off I went to the therapist. It was a very good first session, and I made an appointment to see her again the following week.

When I got home, my mom was sitting in the living room and greeted me with, "So, you're cured now?" I then realized that perhaps I should not be as open with her about everything that was going on in my life.

I told Mom I was fine and never told her again what I did on Tuesday nights. I was in therapy for ten years.

And yes, Mom, now I am cured!

Therapy

I mentioned to a coworker that I was looking for a therapist. She recommended Claire.

Claire's office, comfortably decorated with an air of tranquilly, was on the upper east side of Manhattan. I didn't know what to expect from a therapist, or even what one did in therapy, but I did know that I needed a professional with whom to talk.

Claire is a soft-spoken person with a strong will. During the two years it took to get my divorce, Claire was instrumental in doing what I now know was "emergency" therapy. We never dug deep during those two years; we just worked on getting through each day. She listened as I told her about being terrorized and harassed, and she suggested ways for me to deal with my ex-husband. Claire is a master. She understood me and helped me develop ways to cope. In fact, she sometimes made me practice what I should say when my ex-husband called me at work to harass me. Her tips worked every time.

He would start to call often, beginning early in the evening when I would work late. He played what I call "telephone roulette." He would call and call and call, each time calling a different extension in the office. He knew my extension but would call those of my coworkers in the hope that he could terrorize me and as many of them as possible. It was scary, because I didn't know where he was calling from; he could have been miles away or right downstairs, I just didn't know. When I would answer, he would say nothing until I responded with anxiety and fear.

Claire's tip was that I should simply do the following: in a very calm, monotone voice, I was simply to say, "I have no time for this," and hang up the phone. After the first or second time, that type of call stopped.

During working hours, he would call and rant and rant and rant. I would become emotionally distraught and sometimes cried while I took his verbal abuse, sometimes for a half hour or more.

Claire told me that I should simply say to him in a very calm voice, "I'm looking at my watch, and you have two minutes to tell me exactly what you want, and in two minutes I'm hanging up."

It worked the first time I tried what Claire had taught me, and I never ever got another phone call from him.

Once my divorce was over, I told Claire that I wanted to understand why I allowed myself to be abused and why I allowed it to continue for so long. Claire said, "Fasten your seat belt; it's going to be a rocky ride." Claire was right. But, Claire also told me that within the walls of her office, I could say whatever I wanted to say and know that there would never be judgment. That was the first time in my life I was allowed to say whatever was on my mind. I felt completely safe and cared for in Claire's office. This was a far cry from the realm of omertà that I had lived with all of my life.

Claire and I were together for ten years, and yes, at times it was a rocky road. But it was a road I needed to travel. Claire guided me in understanding how the paradigms I lived with didn't serve me well, omertà being one of them.

I learned from Claire that putting the mirror up to my face, as painful as it sometimes was, was the only way for me to find real happiness.

My Wonderful Wilma

During some of my darkest days, when I was going through my divorce, I had a lot of support from the company's executive officers and my coworkers. One of those coworkers was my assistant, Wilma.

Wilma was my assistant for twelve years. She became my confidante, and she protected me well—very well.

One day there was an incident at the office. My ex-husband showed up unannounced at the security desk in the building lobby and insisted on talking to me in person.

The security desk called my office. Wilma answered, as I was in a meeting. She told security that I was not in and to let my ex-husband know that. She then searched the building for me (I had a habit of letting her know I was going to a meeting but not always saying where—my bad!), and she finally found me.

Wilma is short in physical stature but huge in spirit. She is a no-nonsense, sensible, and outspoken Puerto Rican woman with a heart of gold and an exterior of steel. Thank goodness for me that she had all of those qualities.

Once she found me that day, she assumed control of the situation and insisted that I leave the building once the coast was clear. She called a car service to take me to my mother's house, which was where I was still staying. Then, as if that weren't enough, she went outside the building to wait for the car and called me from the security desk to tell me that it was safe for me to come downstairs. When I came down, she escorted me to the car, and off I went.

I don't think Wilma ever knew how much she may have put herself in harm's way. She just always did what she thought was right.

I will never forget that day or my wonderful, courageous Wilma.

I Have Nothing, or so I Thought

Shortly after I went back to live with my mom, my attorney called to ask me to take inventory of the items in the apartment that I had shared with my ex-husband. To be safe, I asked the bodyguard that I had hired to meet me at my attorney's office (which was a few blocks away from the apartment) and come with me.

As I opened the door of the apartment, my bodyguard and I were both surprised to find that nothing, and I mean nothing, was left there. He had cleaned out the place—except for the shower curtain!

My clothes were gone. All of the furniture was gone. The area rugs were gone. The pots and pans were gone; the books and the bookshelves were gone. The TV was gone. All the dishes and utensils my mother had given me were gone. As I said, everything was gone except for that shower curtain.

After standing in the apartment for a few stunned moments, we left and walked back to my attorney's office. When she saw us walk through her office door, she said, "That was quick." I replied, "Taking inventory is easy when all that's left is a shower curtain."

I had nothing other than the clothes I originally took to my mother's—oh yeah, and a shower curtain. Twenty years worth of stuff was gone.

I was depressed and angry for some time that day, until I realized that I had something more important than "things": I had my freedom.

Two Special People

After the shock of my ex-husband taking all my belongings wore off, my attorney got to work trying to get back the things my mom had given me. Mom had given me my beautiful dinnerware, silverware, and crystal as a wedding present, and I wanted it back (so did my mother!). I didn't really hold out any hope of ever getting it back, but after many months, my attorney was able to arrange to have those things returned to me.

My husband agreed to have it sent to my Aunt Jean and Uncle Mike's house. Aunt Jean and Uncle Mike were always there for me, too. And now that I was going through this horrendous time, they really stood up for me. They not only stored my things but also had to endure a visit from my ex-husband, who delivered my things to their house himself.

The affection I feel for both of them is something I cherish. During the time I lived with my mom, I visited them a lot. Uncle Mike and I would share a glass of wine and talk about so many different things. I always loved talking with them.

In the midst of being stalked, harassed, and threatened, Aunt Jean and Uncle Mike's house was a place where I could laugh and smile and not have to think about the troubles I was facing. Visiting them was like a vacation for my mind.

Thank you, Aunt Jean and Uncle Mike!

Coming Out of the Cave and into the Light

In the "Allegory of the Cave," Plato likens people to prisoners chained in a cave who are only able to look forward. All they can see is the wall in front of them. Behind them burns a fire. Between the fire and the prisoners is a partition, along which puppeteers perform. The puppeteers hold up puppets that cast shadows on the wall of the cave. The prisoners can't see the real objects: the puppets that pass behind them. What the prisoners see are shadows. Illusion is the prisoners' reality.

When the prisoners come out of the cave, they are blinded by the light and need time for their eyes to adjust. So, too, do they need time to adjust to reality.

Release fear! Allow passion, joy, intelligence and humor
to infuse every cell of your being!
...Michael Bernard Beckwith

Fireworks for Me

It was the Fourth of July 1992, seven months after I had left my ex-husband, and we were battling in court.

In order to help me get my mind off my personal problems, my friend Linda asked me if I wanted to spend the day with her at New York's South Street Seaport. Each Fourth of July, New York presents a great fireworks show on the East River, and the Seaport is the perfect place to watch it.

We found a spot that was perfect for viewing, and at 9 PM, the show began. As the fireworks went off, I suddenly felt like a weight had been lifted off me. It was a "lightness" that I had never felt. It was like the fireworks were celebrating my accomplishment of summoning the courage to leave my husband.

I stood there, smiling, and finally knew that while the road ahead was going to be difficult, the journey would be wonderful. I finally realized that I would be able to create the life I wanted, a life free of violence and fear.

The Sea Monster Is Coming for Me

I was living on my own, and my divorce was not yet finalized. As the battle raged, it always seemed like the process would never end. And I began to have a recurring nightmare.

I love to swim in the ocean, but I was always afraid of drowning. I never liked it when the waves were big. In this dream, I was swimming in the water, and all of a sudden, the waves got so big and rough that I was being pulled underwater. If that wasn't enough, a gigantic sea creature that looked like a huge snake appeared (I also don't like snakes).

The waves were bashing me around, and the sea creature kept coming after me. The sea creature would get close, and I would just barely be able to swim out of its way. The dream seemed to go on for hours.

The dream stopped when I woke up. For quite some time, I slept with the lights on as if that would keep me safe from the water and the monster. I thought that if the lights were on, I wouldn't have that stupid nightmare. That didn't work; the dream came with or without the lights on.

Once my divorce was finalized, that dream stopped. I had finally rid myself of the monster.

New Shoes

My ex-husband and I had no children (and no money to speak of), yet it took two years to finalize a divorce.

Our many court visits were a complete waste of time, as he wouldn't agree to anything.

The second time I had to go to court was especially frightful. I was already waiting in the hallway outside of the courtroom with my attorney. My ex-husband came out of the elevator and made a beeline for me. He was moving so deliberately that my attorney thought he was going to attack me. He stepped in, and my husband walked away. We were in court for more than two hours that day to see if my husband would agree to terms. He didn't, and we were finally told to go. So, off I went to work. I was angry, frustrated, and depressed with the idea in my head that our divorce would never get finalized.

As many women in New York City do, I usually wore flats to make it easier on my feet to walk through the city. I kept "work shoes" (high heels) in a drawer in my office. When I got to the office, I opened the "shoe drawer," as I called it, and looked at my shoes. For some reason (probably because they were all bought during my marriage), those pairs of shoes reminded me of him. I got my trash basket and threw them all away.

As I was throwing the shoes out, my boss walked past my office and saw what I was doing and asked Wilma what was going on. She looked at him from her cubicle and simply said, "She's throwing her shoes out." He then said something about that not being a good day to bother me!

When I came into the office the next morning, I opened my shoe drawer as usual to get my business shoes. Of course, I'd forgotten that I had no shoes there anymore.

So, I got up and walked out of my office with my purse and started to let Wilma know where I was going when she interjected, "I know, you are going to buy some new shoes."

New shoes—new life …

The Price of Freedom

I paid my husband. We had been battling for almost two years, primarily because he did not want a divorce. I was the breadwinner; he was unemployed.

One day I'd finally had it. I called the attorney and said "I don't care whether *he* wants a divorce or not; I just want nothing to do with him." And, I told my attorney, "If I see him on the street, I won't even acknowledge him. I will pass him like he doesn't exist."

She contacted his attorney. A few days later, she called me and said that my husband agreed to a divorce, provided I give him a certain amount of money in cash. That's right—cash, no check!

I told her it was a done deal and went to the bank and got the money.

I arrived at my attorney's office that same day and was escorted into the conference room, where my husband and his attorney were waiting for me. I handed the bag of cash to my attorney, who counted it, and he then handed it to my husband's attorney, who also counted it. There was the formality of signing a notarized statement attesting to the fact the cash was the correct amount. The money was handed to my husband, and he left the conference room with his attorney.

At the advice of my attorney I waited for about a half hour before I left to be sure it was "clear."

I also had to pay his attorney fees, but I was able to do that with a check.

I was broke, but I was free!

Old Name—New Life

You learn a lot about law when you get a divorce. One of the lessons I learned was that you could not just go back to your maiden name unless it was part of the divorce and decreed by the judge.

If I hadn't mentioned to my attorney in passing that I wanted to revert to using my maiden name, I would still be stuck with his name. Being stuck with his name would have been a constant reminder of the life I had lived, a life I wanted to put behind me.

Becoming Nancy Salamone again allowed me to emotionally break my ties to him and begin the new life I wanted to create for myself, a life without violence and with the freedom to make my own choices. The last sentence of my divorce, "Ordered, Adjudged, and Decreed, that the plaintiff [that was me] may resume her maiden name, to wit Salamone," was for me an important part of the divorce.

In fact, I felt like I was being born again. Salamone may have been my old name, but with the divorce decree, I was born again and went from victim to survivor, and eventually to thriver.

Old name, new life, new person …

In With the Old

My divorce was finalized on February 17, 1993. I was at work when my attorney called me with the great news. It was finally over!

At my company, every officer had their name on their office door. The nameplate holder made it easy to remove the plate and replace it with a new name if the current occupant moved out and a new person moved in.

The moment I finished talking with my attorney, I got out of my chair, ripped the nameplate off the door, put it on the floor by the door jamb, and slammed the door.

The nameplate was smashed to pieces. When I slammed my door, my coworkers, who had been watching and hearing what I was doing, got up and cheered.

The next day, Wilma made sure that my new name was on my office door.

The Scarred Woman

After my divorce, when I was finally living alone in my own apartment, my dreams changed. One, I will never forget.

In this dream, I saw a woman who had the same hairstyle as I did. I didn't see her face, as her back was always turned toward me.

She walked up to a mirror and stopped in front of it. I saw her reflection in the mirror, and to my shock, it was me—but it wasn't me.

It was certainly my face, but the face and neck in the mirror were horribly scarred. I kept looking at my scarred face; I even put my hand on my face to touch the scars. I was not at all afraid of seeing myself scarred. In fact, I was more fascinated and curious but not afraid. I also didn't think that the scars made me grotesque, even though they were shockingly ugly. I also remember a feeling of complete calm. When I woke up, I was refreshed and happy.

I'm not a therapist or anyone who has knowledge about how to analyze dreams, so I can only presume that I accepted that I had been scarred emotionally and was on my way to healing.

Hip, hip, hooray for me!

The Raging Storms

After my divorce, my first apartment was a small studio in Manhattan. I was living alone and enjoying the solitude. If I wanted to eat cookies for dinner, I did. If I wanted to sleep all day on a weekend, I did. If I wanted to go to dinner with friends, I did that too. If I wanted to go sightseeing in NYC, I did, or if I wanted to do nothing at all, that's what I did. For the first time in my life, I was able to do what I wanted when I wanted to do it.

One wintry Saturday evening there was a storm raging, and I decided to stay home. The storm started in the late afternoon and was predicted to last late into the evening. I was basically just hanging out, enjoying my alone time, when it started.

All of a sudden, my mind became flooded with the times my ex-husband abused me. Every incident deluged my mind in exact detail. This kept up for hours.

I tried to meditate, but that didn't work. I took a warm bath, but that didn't work either. I lit candles and prayed, but the thoughts still didn't stop. I did some exercise, and that didn't work either. I then poured a glass of wine, and even that didn't help.

I gave up and let the horror movie that was my old life play out in my head. The storm outside raged, and so did the storm in my mind. I finally went to bed and just allowed my mind to do what my mind was going to do.

I finally fell into a restless sleep sometime on Sunday morning, and when I woke later, I was exhausted. I rested on Sunday so that I would be able to function at work on Monday.

Thankfully, I never experienced that kind of mental assault again. In fact, I was a much calmer person from then on. I was in the process of letting it all go.

Uh-Oh, What's That Strange Feeling?

I had been in therapy for about two and a half years and wanted to go further.

With Claire's help, I put the mirror up to my face and started to look at why I had married an abusive man and why I stayed with him for so long. Over the next several years, Claire guided me to becoming a person who is strong and capable and *feeling*. Why am I emphasizing feeling? I'll tell you.

I was at home in my studio apartment alone one night, watching television. All of a sudden, I started getting a tingling feeling going through my body. My first thought was that I was coming down with a cold or something. I had never had a feeling like that and could only think that there was something physically wrong with me.

The feeling went away, and on my next visit with Claire, I told her what happened. She smiled a bright smile and said, "Nancy you are finally awakening to your feelings. For so many years, you have shut your feelings off, and now that tingling feeling is your feelings coming back to life."

Moving Day

February 1, 1993, was the day I moved into the first apartment that was truly mine. I was finally on my own at age thirty-nine. It was a great day. It was a snowy, wintry New York City day, but I was so happy.

My friend Linda helped me move. Linda had a small car, and all that I had in the world fit into that little Honda. I only had my clothes and nothing else. I had purchased a convertible couch and a TV, both of which were to be delivered the next day. That night I slept on a comforter on the floor. I didn't mind; I was on my own.

On the way to the apartment, I said to Linda that it was sad that all I had was my clothes. Linda's reply was, "Don't worry; you will have stuff in your next place." She was right. The next place I moved to was a one-bedroom apartment I purchased, and yes, I had things to move besides my clothes.

I may have not had much in the way of things, but I had a new life now!

My Haven

Work had always been my haven. At work, I was respected, heard, trusted, rewarded, and safe. My coworkers and the executives I worked with allowed me to be the creative and competent person that I am. I thrived at work.

When my ex-husband started harassing me, my coworkers and executive officers rallied around me to keep me safe. Not one of them complained or blamed me for what my ex-husband was doing. Instead, they came up with solutions to help keep me and them safe.

In fact, after I separated from my ex-husband, I was promoted to vice president. I will always be grateful for the support and help I received from everyone at the company.

I loved going to work; it was the one place I always felt safe and respected.

The Business of Me

Nobody can go back and start a new beginning, but anyone can start today and make a new ending.
Maria Robinson, Author

Fear Takes Over

Once my divorce was final and I was finally comfortable that he was gone, my new overarching fear became money.

One day, during an intense corporate budget meeting, it dawned on me that the decisions I made in business were just that—business decisions. I knew that I made decisions every day that would help further the goals of the corporation, and I realized that I could bring that way of thinking into my personal life. I also realized that I needed more than just a way to handle my money. I needed a way to use money to attain the life that I wanted.

As soon as the meeting was over, I went back to my office and labeled a folder "The Business of Me."

The first entry in the new file was a list of the things I wanted in my life. It included an idea of what kind of home I wanted and my ideas about where I saw my career going. I wrote down what kind of relationships I wanted, how many vacations I would take each year, the type of friends I wanted, and even the clothes and jewelry I fancied in my life.

What I had done was to outline a vision for my life. Once I had my vision clear, I began developing a plan that would lead me to attaining my new goals.

By now, you might be saying, "Great. Nancy made her list, and off she went into her perfect life." Wrong!

I made my list and went right into panic mode. My old friend fear came back, and I froze and went into a deep depression.

Overcoming Fear

I realized that the fear I felt came from what I was thinking and that if I wanted to change my life, I needed to change the way I thought about things.

While I was a successful corporate officer, in my personal life I was always told that I wasn't good enough or competent enough, so I never thought that I was capable of taking charge of the management of my own life choices and personal finances.

Fortunately, after a few weeks I calmed down and realized that the thing I had to conquer was my own fear. I asked myself, "How am I going to go about moving away from fear?"

"Competent Business Nancy" was the person I was at work, the trusted person who could dazzle her coworkers with her can-do attitude, creativity and ability.

"Fearful Nancy" was the person inside of me, who would freeze with fear and was unable to move forward.

Competent Business Nancy had already been able to create a successful business career and always knew what to do. So, whenever Fearful Nancy showed up, I asked her to leave so that Competent Business Nancy could take charge.

I then called on Competent Business Nancy, and as I did with every business issue I dealt with, I did research. My first stop was the dictionary to find out what fear really is.

The Webster's Dictionary that I had in my office described fear as, "a feeling of disquiet or apprehension, a distressing emotion aroused by impending danger, evil, or pain—whether the threat is real or imagined." Whether real or imagined ...

Fear, I also learned, is a basic survival mechanism that occurs in response to a specific stimulus, such as pain or the threat of pain or violence.

Now I knew what fear felt like, what fear was, and how it can be real or imagined.

Every time I was fearful, it felt like I'd been punched in the stomach. I felt fear to the point I could not eat, and when I did eat, the food wouldn't stay in my stomach. Fear was a great weight loss program for me … but that's it!

Where Fear Starts

Now I knew what fear was, but I asked myself, "Where is it coming from?"

As I walked around each day asking myself that question, I finally realized that the fear I felt was because of what I was imagining: *I was scaring myself.* I realized that the fear I felt was coming from my imagination without any outside stimulus. The fear existed only in my mind.

Once I realized that it was my own fearful thoughts that kept me in this state, I set out to do something about it.

Thank goodness for Competent Business Nancy. She got up and went off to a stationary store and bought a small notebook.

At work, I always carried a notebook to record notes or thoughts I had about how to further the goals of the company.

My good friend and one of my best teachers, Marty Smith, told me once, "Whatever you are thinking, the opposite is probably true."

I thought about what Marty had taught me and began writing down all the things that made me afraid. Next to it, I wrote an opposite thought—a positive affirmation—to counter the negative one.

I did this for many weeks, and to my amazement, I found that my depression was lifting. I had more energy. I felt better about myself and was finally ready to move on to tackling the real work of attaining my vision.

What I had begun was a process of kicking negative self-talk out of my life and replacing it with positive self-talk.

Creating The Business of Me

Since my file was titled "The Business of Me," and because I felt so competent in business, I decided to make "me" a company, and I gave my company a name.

The name I chose was Nancy's Perfect Life, Inc., which allowed me to use Competent Business Nancy's skills and kick Fearful Nancy out of the conversation.

Competent Business Nancy knew that for a company to be successful, it needed a capable CEO at its helm. So, I signed a contract with Nancy's Perfect Life, Inc., and became its CEO.

I placed the signed contract on my refrigerator door so I could see it and refer to it. That contract became my motivator and helped me to do the work that was necessary for Nancy's Perfect Life, Inc., to be successful. I also agreed to pay the bills of the company on a timely basis and not ignore them.

You see, Fearful Nancy was a master of sticking her head in the sand when it came to paying bills, so she needed to stay out of the bill-paying process.

Because I was a corporate executive, I knew that, as CEO, I was responsible for the financial health of my company. As a businessperson, I knew that the next step was to develop a workable budget. Fearful Nancy thought budgets were like diets: "You have been bad, so now you have to deprive yourself." But Competent Business Nancy knew a budget was a tool that could help move a company toward its goals.

Developing The Business of Me Budget

My first step was to research the components of a personal budget and to then develop the budget based on my income and expenses.

Competent Business Nancy also knew that a corporate budget was designed to meet current monthly needs and to project future needs as well.

For example, Nancy's Perfect Life, Inc., wanted to purchase a home, so the budgeting would need to include setting aside money for that purpose.

I did a lot of research about what format to use in creating my budget. As a matter of fact, the budget form used today for The Business of Me is very similar to the budget form Competent Business Nancy used to manage Nancy's Perfect Life, Inc., more than fifteen years ago.

The research that I found gave me some great tips, like keep the budget simple. This means you should not clutter it with too many categories. For example, while I needed to know how to estimate my variable weekly expenses, I did not need to keep track of every little purchase I made; I only needed to keep track of "total miscellaneous" items, which might include whatever day-to-day purchases I made.

Fearful Nancy liked that approach, because she knew that if things became too complicated, she could and would abandon the process!

It took over a month for me to perfect the budget for Nancy's Perfect Life, Inc., but once it was done, I had a road map to follow for my company, for me, for my life!

Networking My Way to Financial Self-Sufficiency

The next step in my process was to learn about money and personal money management. I could manage large sums of corporate money, but I needed to learn how to manage my own.

Competent Business Nancy decided to tap into her resources. Fortunately, I was able to find women who were experts in personal finance, and I set up meetings with them. I learned a lot from them about handling and investing money. Besides learning about concepts like "variable" and "fixed" expenses, I learned about setting up an emergency fund and where the money comes from to do that. I implemented the suggestions these women gave me. With their help, I was on the road to achieving what I envisioned for my life.

One of the most important lessons I learned from them was about the power of networking, so I found a group of women that I could meet with to talk about personal finances and how to manage money.

There were six of us in the group. We met monthly to discuss our money issues and learn from one another about various personal financial management strategies. The group acted as the board of directors for Nancy's Perfect Life, Inc., giving me sound advice and providing the support that I needed. Today, The Business of Me program incorporates a powerful continuing support group through the board of directors groups and through our Facebook group pages.

Learning to Take Care of Myself

There was another message I was getting from my group and that was how important it is to take time for yourself. Until that point in my life, it was unheard of to take time for me. Now I know that it is not only okay but vitally necessary to take time to do things just for you.

This was a tough concept for Fearful Nancy to accept. I always thought that I had to take care of others, not me! As the sole wage earner in the family, I was used to putting a roof over our heads and food on our table before anything else.

Because the money I was allowed to spend during my marriage was always so regulated, I never did the things that most women do. Although I was a successful businesswoman, my mother cut my hair, I manicured my own nails, and never, never just went shopping. The only money I ever spent on myself then was on Sunday mornings. In order to get out of the house, I would walk over to a nearby bakery and buy myself a scone—for seventy-five cents. That was my one luxury.

After some thought, I decided to give it a whirl! I decided that I would take some time for me and get a facial at a little local spa.

But, you know what? Spending $35 on a facial and doing something for myself gave me a migraine!

Never having taken time for myself, my old negative self-talk came back to tell me that I wasn't worthy and did not *deserve* to take care of myself. Hence, the migraine.

I thought that perhaps the facial might have been too much to start with, so I scaled back to manicures. And, lo and behold, I was able to handle manicures without getting a headache!

As time went on, I learned how to schedule time for myself and enjoy it. I began to understand that I was the most important resource in Nancy's Perfect Life, Inc., and that it was essential that, first and foremost, I take care of me.

Wants vs. Needs

One day, the company I worked for called a meeting of all senior officers. The meeting was held off-site.

Senior management believed that the topic was so important to the future of the company that they wanted us to be away from our usual daily routine so that we could concentrate on just one topic. The topic was the corporation's "wants" versus its "needs."

They requested that we participate in an in-depth discussion of what the company needed to do not only to compete but to overtake the competition. We discussed the role and function of every department, from service areas to operational departments, to find out if what each department did was really absolutely necessary. We questioned everything. Were we doing things that were really required, or were we doing them because someone simply wanted them done?

The executive vice president, who moderated the discussion, wrote two words on the flip chart that he was using that day. Those two words were "wants" and "needs."

He wrote them side by side and then drew a line between them. Next, he asked all of us about what we felt were the wants versus the needs of every operating unit in the company.

A lively discussion ensued, with each of us stating our case for why a routine that our departments did was absolutely necessary or why a new routine was needed. The moderator diligently wrote each comment under the "want" or the "need" side of the flip chart. By the end of that day, after a very robust discussion, we had a complete list of the company's new wants and needs.

The point of relating that story is that Competent Business Nancy realized that if large corporations felt it was vital to understand the difference between their company's wants and needs to move it forward, Nancy's Perfect Life, Inc., needed to know what her wants versus needs were so that she could move forward to achieve her goals.

I wrote on a legal pad the words "wants" and "needs" and drew a line down the middle. I listed each of the things I thought I wanted and needed under its appropriate heading. Then I began to analyze each of them.

For example, in the want column, I wrote that I would like to take certain courses to earn additional accreditations to advance my career.

After my divorce, I began hoarding money. The flaw in a hoarding mentality, or a "save, save, save" belief, is that it inhibits activities such as further education that might actually lead to earning more money so that I could have more of the things I wanted in my life. I did the same exercise that we did at the meeting and ended with my new list of wants versus my needs.

My Values Assessment

As I was working my plan, I continued with my networking meetings each month.

One month, a woman in the group, a life coach, suggested that we do an exercise that would help us better understand our values. She told us that if we understood what our values were, we could better understand what we wanted from life.

The exercise began with each of us writing down the names of people we admire and the traits in them we admired. We were told that the people we admire did not have to be famous or wealthy. The names I chose were only recognizable to me: Zelda, Roberta, and Harriett.

Zelda and Roberta were partners in a insurance and securities brokerage firm that they founded and called Financial Women.

"Financial women" described Zelda and Roberta perfectly. They were financial experts in all aspects of insurance, stocks and bonds, wealth management, estate planning, and IRS rules and regulations. Their clients were men and women who were well off and needed experienced, qualified advice and money management.

When people met Zelda and Roberta, they would think that they were entirely different from one another. Zelda was outspoken and direct, while Roberta was diplomatic and soft-spoken. Yet, both had many similar qualities. Both were generous, courageous, bold, inquisitive, analytical, curious, fashionable, outgoing, and social—all qualities that I admired. I was so fortunate that these women took me under their wing and became my mentors.

Harriett has the most loving heart and generous soul of any person I have ever met. She has an unlimited capacity to care about other people, yet she is the most street-smart and savvy woman I have ever known. She's also tough.

I know "tough" is not a word many people like to use to describe a woman, but the complex businesses that these women were involved in required toughness.

When I say tough, I mean standing by one's convictions, a trait that I admired in all three of them. I learned from them that it is acceptable to speak my mind—provided I have the facts to back up my statements.

Once we completed the exercise that day, the life coach told us that the qualities we admired in those people were, in fact, qualities that we already had within ourselves. It shocked me to realize that those were qualities I already possessed, and all I had to do was choose to acknowledge them in myself.

After all, I was a corporate officer. I could not have achieved what I had if I didn't possess the qualities of strength that I admired in others. Having been constantly told I was worthless by my ex-husband, it never occurred to me that I was a competent, intelligent, and compassionate woman like Zelda, Roberta, and Harriett.

Today I would add two other women to that list who have had a great influence on my life: Dede Bartlett and Carole Hyatt. Both women have opened their networks to me and allowed me to be part of their lives. Both are successful businesswomen and have always assisted other women in achieving their potential.

These are the kind of women all women need in their lives.

Ready to Give Back

Some years passed, and I was in a place where I wanted to give back. I have been very fortunate.

By then, The Business of Me was operative in my life. I had bought my own home survived breast cancer, and I had even bought myself a mink coat and a Rolex watch. I had traveled to the Caribbean, Italy, Mexico, France, Spain, Sicily, Hawaii, and the Czech Republic. And by then, I knew not only how devastating it was to live in a violent relationship but also how difficult it is to leave the relationship and create a life for oneself. But, I was experiencing the joy in my life that independence brought me.

Millions of women like me have to learn good money management skills, especially women who have left or are in the process of leaving an abusive relationship. For them, these skills are essential in breaking free of the recurring cycle of domestic violence.

Carole Hyatt is an accomplished author, speaker, and businesswoman. Carole leads seminars for women executives, and one day I was fortunate enough to be invited to attend one of her seminars.

After the seminar, I approached Carole, introduced myself, and told her I wanted to help women who, like me, had left violent relationships. Carole didn't hesitate and immediately told me to call Dede Bartlett. At that time, Dede was corporate secretary of a Fortune 100 company and chair of the New York City Domestic Violence Council.

I called Dede and told her what I wanted to do, and she immediately invited me to attend the next meeting of the council. The council included members of the corporate community, executives from women's organizations, and members of the legal and judicial communities. All of these people had a common goal: to help women get out and stay out of domestic violent relationships.

After one meeting, I spoke to Dede and told her about my goal to develop a program for women survivors of domestic violence to help them achieve financial self-sufficiency.

Dede wasted no time and called over a woman named Mary Baughman, who is the executive director of Jersey Battered Women's Services. Mary just happened to be looking for a financial self-sufficiency program for the women in her shelter in Morristown, New Jersey.

Mary and I met several times, and I explained that these women would need to address their fears about managing their own finances in order to obtain the personal financial management skills they needed to break the cycle of violence. Mary agreed, and I wrote the program called, "The Business of Me." Since then, I have moderated The Business of Me groups all over the northeastern United States.

The Business of Me Evolves

So that The Business of Me can be brought to women all over the country, we've now written the program so that it can be presented by staff within organizations nationwide. This makes it possible to present The Business of Me to any organization anywhere anytime they have a group ready to go.

The program, which is presented over a six-week period, is followed by the monthly board of directors meetings and continually supported through our Social Networking pages. The program includes more than just real-world personal financial management skills. It includes all that I have learned about how to break fears surrounding money and money management through what the program calls "self-ability."

The Program

During the first weekly session, the participants are asked to open a page in the binder of materials that is provided to each of them. They are asked to draw a line down the middle of the page and, on one side, write down their negative self-talk and put the corresponding positive affirmation that negates it in the opposite column. They then tear the negative self-talk out of their binders, leaving only the positive affirmations on which they can now concentrate. The pages of negative self-talk are burned as a symbol of releasing the negative thoughts. This exercise is repeated before each session of The Business of Me.

The program then teaches participants how to do a values assessment, how to recognize their wants and their needs, and how to use real-world financial skills, including the budget process that I mentioned previously. This includes identifying fixed, variable, and discretionary spending, with detailed information about each item and tips about how to save on each expense.

Participants are taught the importance of acquiring, reading, and understanding a credit report and how to understand a personal credit score. The program goes on to explain various types of insurance and what a 401(k) is and what it's for. More budget-stretching ideas, such as saving on insurance, grocery, and other purchases, are presented.

We teach bankruptcy as a last resort, the ramifications of filing one, and how to recover from it.

Many of our participants are mothers. The program emphasizes the importance of teaching their children good financial management and "giving back" skills early in life and how to give the children increasing responsibility for their own financial lives as they mature.

We then teach our participants the process of creating a personal "SWOT" analysis to help them analyze their *s*trengths, *w*eaknesses, *o*pportunities, and the *t*hreats that they might face in attaining their aspirations. We teach them to use this tool continually to plan for their future.

The first three board of directors' support group meetings are held in the organization's facilities and chaired by the same moderator who presented the program. At the close of the third meeting, the group elects a permanent chairperson, who then leads the group for its first year. Thereafter, the group elects a new chairperson yearly, and the group continues to support its members long into the future.

We've created a Facebook group page (Facebook The Business of Me) and create individual Facebook group pages for each group of participants to help them learn from one another. These Facebook groups support the work of the board of directors and to offer participants and moderators additional support and services online.

And, finally, we provide many resources on our Website for our participants and friends to use. They include ways to save money and a list of places to get coupons and rebates online. It's all at www.thebusinessofme.com.

The Business of Me Today

That some achieve great success is proof to all that others can achieve it as well.

...Abraham Lincoln

Success!

We have seen wonderful results from The Business of Me. The program works.

The Business of Me teaches real-world financial management skills and doable day-to-day techniques to help women achieve financial self-sufficiency.

I have had the privilege of presenting The Business of Me to countless women. During the years, I have seen women who were afraid to speak up when they entered the program become animated as the session's progress. I have seen women who did not care about themselves begin to take care of themselves. I have seen women who were afraid become empowered. I have seen women who felt as if they were stupid realize they are intelligent, productive members of society. I have seen women create lasting friendships. I have seen women thrive in ways that are wonderful!

I cannot begin to describe the personal joy that I've received from presenting this program. As the weekly sessions progress, it is pure pleasure to watch the women become enthusiastic and begin to develop a "can-do" and an "I want to do it" attitude.

I would like to tell you about the effectiveness of The Business of Me through the stories of two women in the program, who I will call Kelly and Teresa.

Kelly's Story

To say that Kelly is beautiful is an understatement. Kelly is "movie star" beautiful; in fact, she looks like Nicole Kidman. Yet, Kelly did not feel beautiful outside or inside. She was, at the age of thirty-three, a survivor of domestic violence and of breast cancer; she had undergone a full mastectomy.

Kelly told me that she was a breast cancer survivor, because, during my introduction, I told the group that I was both a domestic violence and breast cancer survivor.

During a break, she came to tell me she was just like me. Kelly sounded so relieved that she had met another person who shared an experience similar to hers.

There was a wonderful moment with Kelly when we were doing the values assessment exercise. The exercise requests that the participants write the names of people they admire and the traits they admire in those people. During the sharing part of the exercise, Kelly told the group that she admired her aunt, since she had two traits that Kelly greatly admired. One trait was courage, and the other was her resilience. I pointed out to Kelly that she also had those traits, and she looked astonished. I said softly, "Kelly, you have left a domestic violent relationship and survived breast cancer. Of course you are not only courageous but also resilient." Kelly started to cry and said it had never occurred to her that she had those traits. Later, during the break, Kelly said she was now ready to do the work she needed to get her financial life in order, because if she had survived both domestic violence and breast cancer, she could do that, too.

Teresa's Story

Teresa lives in a small town and has been one of the recipients of services from a local domestic violence shelter. At one time, she had a workable and responsible life. She had been a manager at the postal service, supervised between fifteen and twenty-five people, and owned her own home.

Then, life took an unexpected turn. A man walked into her life and turned it upside down. He was handsome, socially adept, and fun. But, he was no prince, and they did not create a fairy-tale ending. She, eventually, lost her home, her job, and any stability from her former life. Remembering what happened still infuriated her.

"He walked into my life, and I thought, this is fun, and I don't have to be responsible. Even though I was the breadwinner and owned the house, I somehow allowed him to take over. When he told me I couldn't balance the checkbook, I even bought that. In the face of violence and threats, I kept denying that anything bad was happening to me. You know, sometimes it seems amazing, even to me, that I got myself into this mess."

Fortunately, she began talking with an advocate with whom she found the courage to describe what was happening to her. She finally left the relationship and became a part of the program at the shelter. She feels grateful to them as well as the post office personnel.

"The post office officials were key in advocating for me and getting me a therapist. They followed the procedures outlined for survivors of domestic violence. They really tried to help me for years. Finally, I went on disability. I suffered from post-traumatic stress. I had no previous medical or psychiatric problems before this mess. I had been a normal, middle-class, American woman with a good head on her shoulders."

Teresa became a participant in The Business of Me through her involvement in the program at the shelter. The program director told Teresa, "Boy, do I have something for you!" Teresa participated in the workshop in September 2004. While she reported getting a lot out of the program, full participation took some courage on her part.

"Some of the experience was hard for me. I wasn't comfortable socially. I had become very secluded as a result of my experience with this man, and I wasn't confident about my social skills. I was reluctant to participate in some of the exercises and activities, because I didn't want to show that I didn't know something. I am the type of person that keeps what I value to myself, because, in the past, whenever I have shown stuff that is valuable, it's been taken from me.

"Nancy presented things in a way that invited participation, or she treated your decision not to participate with complete respect. She didn't make anyone do anything. It was all my choice." The Business of Me created an atmosphere that made these decisions easy for Teresa to make.

Teresa chose not to do several exercises. She did not want to make a collage, because she suffers from a neuropathology that makes handling scissors difficult. When it came to the point in the program to create a name for their personal company, Teresa did not want to, and she did not want to burn negative thoughts and words that she was carrying in her head.

"Nancy either said, 'No problem!' or created another way for me to do something similar. She is very accepting. She is on your level while being professional. You know what really stuck with me was that she was a professional woman, and she talked in a language that was comprehensible but not condescending. And that was inviting me to participate. Most important, everything she used in the classroom you can do at a later time because of all the handouts. So, I walked out of there with something in my hand and in my head, something concrete I could use immediately."

In spite of Teresa's intermittent participation, she felt as though the work had helped her "turn a corner."

Prior to the workshop, she favored avoidance as a strategy for dealing with her money. Now, with the handouts and exercises from the workshop, she felt much more comfortable with the idea that she could control her finances. Since then, she has set up a budget and appreciates its usefulness. She has really mastered something.

Teresa decided to advance her career and enrolled in online courses from the University of Phoenix. She studied accounting (of all things!). She maintains her relationship with the organization by volunteering there to help other survivors with their resumes and helps the administrative staff with the mail.

"I've finally landed on my feet after stumbling along. Nancy walked in at the right time. On one of the worksheets she gave us is a saying: 'Success comes from success.' I think The Business of Me class helped people regard themselves as successful. Nancy gets everyone caught up in the excitement and the sense of possibility. I'm smiling now just telling you about it."

Afterword

Nothing changes until you do.
… Paol Seagram, Author, Artist, Teacher

Acclaimed Yale University anthropologist David Levinson, in a family violence study (*Family Violence in Cross-Cultural Perspective*, Dr. David Levinson, Sage Publications, 1989.) he conducted that focused on battered women, found that in the ninety societies he studied, incidents of battering were practically nonexistent when women have economic independence and support from other women.

And that is what The Business of Me strives to offer women everywhere.

My dark days are long behind me, and I have not just survived, but indeed, I have thrived.

The path to happiness was sometimes a rocky road, but one that was filled with the support of friends and loved ones.

My hope is that women who have endured their own struggles find something from my story and realize that they too can create the financially self-sufficient life that they choose and achieve their own "Victory over Violence".

I'm Nancy Salamone. Please contact me directly at
nancy@thebusinessofme.com

www.thebusinessofme.com
www.nancysstory.com
Facebook: The Business of Me

Acknowledgments

This book would not have been possible if it were not for those who helped me through my darkest times, including Andrea Wolff, my attorney and friend, who I called endlessly during those days and who is, to this day, one of my most trusted friends and advisers.

I will always be grateful to Dr. Claire Ciliotta, who came into my life when I needed her the most and not only helped me through my toughest times but helped me to go from victim to survivor to thriver.

I will always be thankful to Dr. Marvin Zuckerman, who always took such good care of me.

Patricia McCormick, Linda Scenna, Martin Smith, Wilma Rosario, Jo Ann Craner, Karen Rosica, and Stan Hustad have all been instrumental in my life and helped me bring *Victory Over Violence: Nancy's Story and "The Business of Me"* to reality.

To my sister and brother-in-law, who really stood up for me during those dark days; and to Fran Pullano, who recently came back in my life and became a champion of The Business of Me, I will always be grateful.

To Amy and Michael Santullo, who believed in me and made it possible to get this book published, thank you from the bottom of my heart.

Maurice Bretzfield sat next to me and tirelessly edited the book with me. I have no words other than that I will always be thankful that he came into my life.